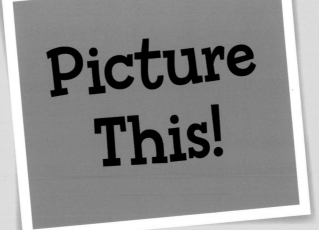

Picture This!

Seasons

Rebecca Rissman

Raintree

Raintree is an imprint of Capstone Global Library Limited, a company incorporated in England and Wales having its registered office at 7 Pilgrim Street, London, EC4V 6LB – Registered company number: 6695582

www.raintreepublishers.co.uk
myorders@raintreepublishers.co.uk

Text © Capstone Global Library Limited 2014
First published in hardback in 2014
First published in paperback in 2015
The moral rights of the proprietor have been asserted.

Edited by Daniel Nunn, Catherine Veitch, and Clare Lewis
Designed by Marcus Bell
Picture research by Liz Alexander
Production by Victoria Fitzgerald
Originated by Capstone Global Library Ltd
Printed and bound in China

ISBN 978 1 406 25961 2 (hardback)
17 16 15 14 13
10 9 8 7 6 5 4 3 2 1

ISBN 978 1 406 25966 7 (paperback)
18 17 16 15 14
10 9 8 7 6 5 4 3 2 1

British Library Cataloguing in Publication Data
A full catalogue record for this book is available from the British Library.

Acknowledgements

We would like to thank the following for permission to reproduce photographs: Corbis p. 16 (© Winfried Wisniewski); Nature Picture Library pp. 3 (© Artur Tabor), 4 (© Steven Kazlowski), 9 (© Artur Tabor); Shutterstock pp. 3 (© Pavel L Photo and Video, © Songchai W, © Matej Ziak), 4 (© Eric Gevaert, © Jason Patrick Ross), 5 (© Marc Norman, © Pavel Vakhrushev), 6 (© Pi-Lens, © Maryna Pleshkun, © Oliver Sved, © gorillaimages), 7 (© Pavel L Photo and Video), 8 (© Ewa Studio, © Monika Gniot, © Marie C Fields), 9 (© 1000 Words, © Steve Byland, © 501room), 10 (© Vasaleks, © Algefoto, © Armadillo Stock), 11 (© Sergiy Bykhunenko, © Roberto Caucino, © kurhan), 12 (© lordcal, © Maksym Gorpenyuk, © IbajaUsap), 13 (© Songchai W), 14 (© Andreas Gradin, © oliveromg, © Brocreative), 15 (© Goodluz), 16 (© Galyna Andrushko, © Yellowj, © Matej Ziak), 17 (© BMJ), 18 (© Gladskikh Tatiana, © Gladskikh Tatiana, © Charles Brutlag, © Gladskikh Tatiana), 19 (© Andrey Armyagov), 23 (© 501room); SuperStock pp. 10 (imagebroker.net), 12 (Marka).

Front cover photograph of goslings reproduced with permission of Shutterstock (© Pakhnyushcha).

Back cover photographs of a girl with an umbrella reproduced with permission of Shutterstock (© Vasaleks).

Every effort has been made to contact copyright holders of material reproduced in this book. Any omissions will be rectified in subsequent printings if notice is given to the publisher.

Contents

Winter

Spring

Summer

Autumn

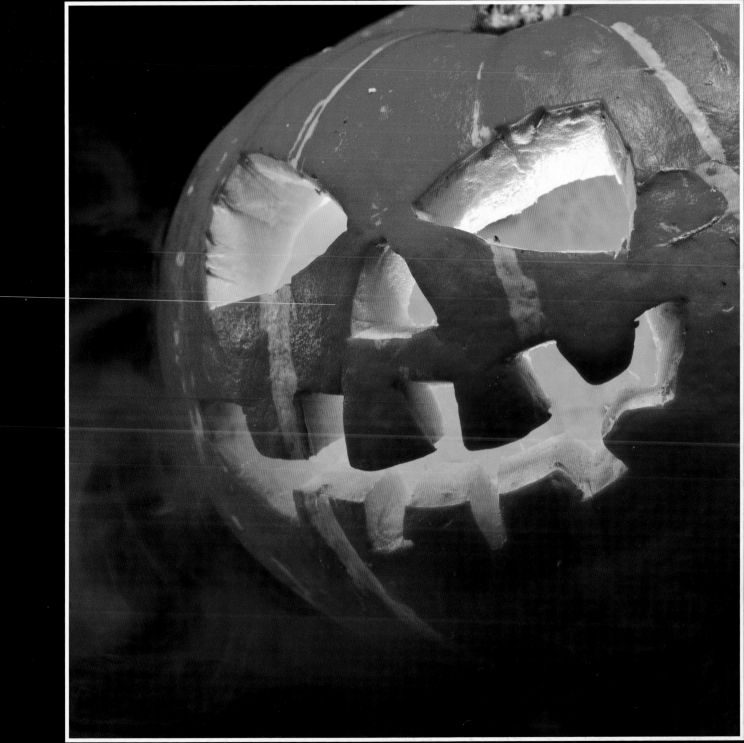

Find out more about the photos

Page 4   Arctic foxes play in Alaska in the top left photo. In the top right photo, a robin rests in the snow. The photo at the bottom of the page shows a snowy hiking trail in Illinois, USA.

Page 5   The photo at the top shows icicles hanging from a frozen ledge. In the bottom right photo, snowdrops grow through the snow.

Page 6   Husky dogs race across a frozen field in the photo at the top of the page. In the bottom left corner, a photo shows two adults shovelling snow. The photo at the bottom centre of the page shows a woman using an umbrella in a blizzard. In the bottom right corner, two children sledge down a hill.

Page 7   This photo shows a boy making a large snowman.

Page 8   Cherry blossoms (left) and tulips (right) bloom in the top two photos. At the bottom, a mother mallard duck cares for her new ducklings.

Page 9   A photo of blooming cherry trees appears at the top left of the page. The top right photo shows two newborn lambs. In the bottom left photo, a bird's nest holds four eggs. The bottom right photo shows a field of blooming flowers.

Page 10   The top three photos on this page show children dressed for rain, with umbrellas, welly boots, and a rain coat. At the bottom of the page, a young girl in Germany feeds a donkey in the spring.

Page 11 Two photos on this page show people riding bikes outdoors in the springtime. The photo at the bottom right shows two children digging in the garden during the spring.

Page 12 A ladybird, a dragonfly, and a butterfly appear in photos on this page. In the bottom right photo, a large deer walks through a forest.

Page 13 Beautiful sunflowers grow in a sunny field in the summertime.

Page 14 The photo at the top of this page shows two children playing football in Sweden. In the bottom left photo, a family enjoys a summer barbecue. The bottom right photo shows children playing in the sea.

Page 15 This photo shows a family enjoying a summer day at the beach.

Page 16 The photo at the top of the page shows beautiful autumn trees. At the bottom of the page, photos show a squirrel gathering nuts, geese migrating south for the winter, and a hedgehog nestled in fallen leaves.

Page 17 This photo shows a dormouse curled up in fallen leaves.

Page 18 The photos at the top of this page show children playing in fallen leaves. At the bottom left, a photo shows a father and son enjoying an evening bonfire. At the bottom right, two carved Halloween pumpkins light up a porch.

Page 19 A carved Halloween lantern glows brightly in this large photo.

Discussion questions

Page 4 shows photos of animals during the winter.

What other animals are outdoors during the winter?

Why might it be difficult for animals to find water in winter?

Some animals use thick fur and feathers to stay warm during cold winter months. Others stay warm in burrows or nests.

Can you think of any other ways animals stay warm during the winter?

Page 5 shows an image of a snowdrop growing through the snow.

What other plants do you see growing in the winter?

Do you see many flowers in the winter?

Pages 6–7 show some wintertime activities.

What other activities, sports, or games can you think of that people do during the winter?

What is your favourite thing to do outdoors during the winter?

Do you enjoy it when it snows?

Why do some people *not* like snow very much?

Pages 8–9 show some young animals and plants in the spring.

What other young animals and plants might you see in the spring?

Weather in the spring can be warm and mild.

Why do you think many animals are born during the spring?

Page 10 shows people dressed for rain.

Is it always rainy in the spring?

What other types of weather might you experience during the spring?

Page 11 shows some activities that you can do in the spring.

Why is spring a good time to go cycling?

Is it better to do gardening in the winter or the spring?

What could you plant in the spring?

Pages 12–13 show different plants and animals in the summer.

Can you think of any other plants and animals you might see during the summer?

What things can you do in summer that you can't do in the winter?

Summer weather is usually warm or hot with lots of sun.

Do you think plants grow better during the summer or winter?

Pages 14–15 show people enjoying the weather in the summer.

Is it warm or cold where you live during the summer?

What activities do you like to do in the summer?

Pages 16–17 show plants and animals in the autumn.

How do trees look different in the autumn?

What animals do you see during the autumn?

Some animals prepare to hibernate (sleep through the winter) during the autumn. How do animals prepare?

Squirrels and bears hibernate.
Can you think of any other animals that hibernate?

Page 18 shows children playing in leaves during the autumn.

What other activities do you like to do during the autumn?

Is the weather warm or cold where you live in the autumn?

Index